IMAGES
of America

WESTPORT

IMAGES
of America

WESTPORT

Westport Museum for History & Culture

ARCADIA
PUBLISHING

Published by Arcadia Publishing
Charleston, South Carolina

Printed in the United States of America

Library of Congress Control Number: 2019954313

For all general information, please contact Arcadia Publishing:
Telephone 843-853-2070
Fax 843-853-0044
E-mail sales@arcadiapublishing.com
For customer service and orders:
Toll-Free 1-888-313-2665

Visit us on the Internet at www.arcadiapublishing.com

Westport Museum for History & Culture acknowledges that Westport was founded upon exclusions and erasures of the native Paugusset peoples upon whose original land this institution is located.

CONTENTS

Acknowledgments   6

Introduction   7

1.   Liberty to Set Down   9

2.   Westport in the Revolution and Early Republic   15

3.   Westport Becomes an Independent Town   19

4.   Industry, Innovation, and Industrialists   23

5.   Around the Town   45

6.   Recreation   93

7.   Westport in the Arts   121

ACKNOWLEDGMENTS

Westport Museum for History & Culture gratefully acknowledges the efforts of its staff and volunteer researchers, past and present, whose work has made this book possible. Archives manager Sara Krasne's extensive knowledge of Westport's history and the holdings in our collection allowed us to carefully curate the photos you find here and which we believe offer the greatest view of the town over time. Our executive director, Ramin Ganeshram, was kind enough to lend her professional writing expertise to this project, and we are most appreciative.

We also wish to thank Charles Reimer, the grandson of Dr. Frederick Ruland, who has been most generous in the loan of family photographs taken by his grandmother Leo that provide a unique view into Westport at the turn of the 20th century. The research done by Joanna Foster for her book *Stories from Westport's Past*, first published in 1985, was also invaluable for reconstructing the stories that accompanied associated images.

The work of preserving the precious images that are highlighted in this volume has been a labor of love for those many individuals who came before us at the Westport Historical Society, now Westport Museum. Their passion for history and love of the town and organization continue to be the foundation upon which we work to share the exciting and engaging history of our town.

Unless otherwise noted, all images appear courtesy of the Westport Museum for History & Culture.

INTRODUCTION

What is today the town of Westport was originally the holding of Machumux, Saugatuck, and Norwalk natives of the Paugusset nation who had inhabited the area for at least 7,500 years before English colonizers arrived in the 17th century. Situated on the shores of Long Island Sound and at the mouth of the Saugatuck River, the area was ideally placed for farming, fishing, and commerce. It comprised both the towns of Fairfield and Norwalk with the Saugatuck River as the dividing line between.

What would become Westport began in 1648 when a group of Fairfield farmers established the "West Parish" of their town at the shoreline of Green's Farms. In 1825, nearly 200 years after that original Green's Farms settlement, the Town of Westport was formally incorporated as a distinct municipality at the urging of men like Daniel Nash and others.

In the following decades, Westport would evolve from a farming and shipping community into a factory town, a bucolic retreat for both wealthy robber barons and the common man, an enclave for artists and performers, and finally, a bedroom community for New York City. Through the centuries, Westport has been at the forefront of technological innovation, social flux, and shifting population patterns.

Each era of Westport's evolution has left an indelible imprint, ultimately creating a town with a unique character formed by both larger-than-life and everyday citizens who called Westport home. In this book, you will find their stories told through the images of their lives and times.

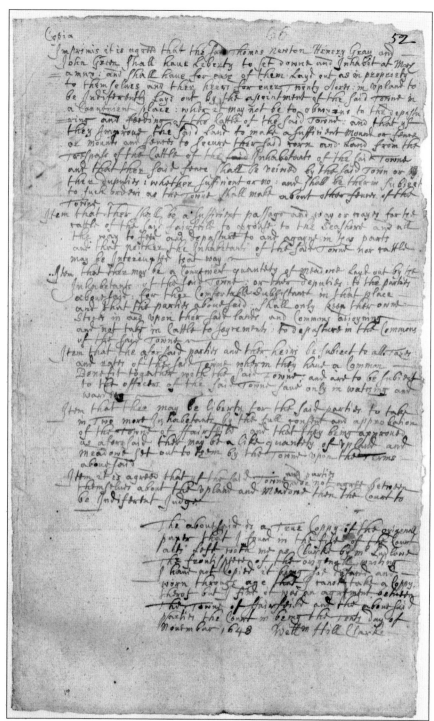

The original 1648 grant to settle the area that would become the Green's Farms section of Westport was for 20 acres given to Thomas Newton, Henry Gray, and John Green, "indifferently layd out by the appointment of said Towne in a convenient place." Later joined by other families, the group became known as the Bankside Farmers.

One

LIBERTY TO SET DOWN

In 1648, English-born Thomas Newton, Henry Gray, and John Green, later known as the Bankside Farmers, were granted "liberty to set down and inhabit" the land that would later be commonly known as "Green's Farms"—the core of Westport.

The area had been called Machamux, or "beautiful land," by the Paugusset Nation natives from the Saugatuck and Machamux tribes who had lived there. Most of the tribe's members had been massacred 11 years earlier in the Great Swamp Fight between themselves and the English in the Sasco Creek marshlands between Westport and Fairfield. According to local lore, the remaining captives were moved to the area of Westport at Clapboard Hill Road in what was one of the earliest Indian reservations in the state. Others were enslaved, joining Africans as a key commodity for the Bankside Farmers as well as for others in the parts of Norwalk and Fairfield that would come together to form the town of Westport in 1835. These forced migrants from Africa labored in the fields, on the shores, and in the homes of early Westport, bringing prosperity to those who held them captive.

Colonial Westport, like other harbor towns, was active in the trade between the North American colonies and the Caribbean. Crops such as corn, wheat, and flax were grown and milled at the Sherwood Mill. From there, they were sent to warehouses lining the river in the town of Saugatuck—now downtown Westport. Goods were then loaded onto small ships headed for New York or Boston and then on to trade in the Caribbean or Europe in return for sugar, rum, and enslaved peoples.

Like their counterparts in other colonies, Westport men were loyal Britons, and many served in the French and Indian War (Seven Year's War) only to return to face higher taxes from Parliament to pay for the extended military engagement. Westport's businessmen and farmers suffered the economic hardships of higher taxes on paper, sugar, and tea, which would eventually lead them to support the War for Independence.

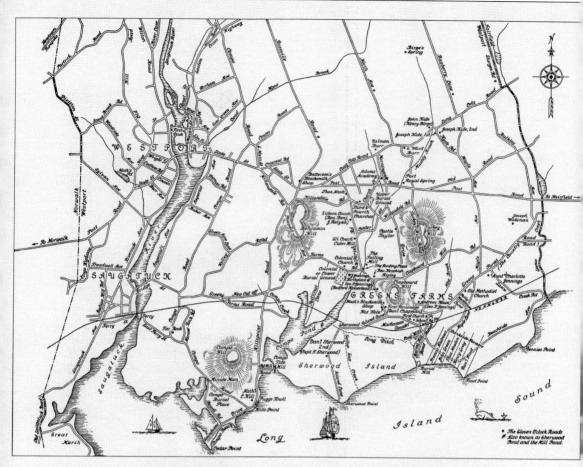

WESTPORT, GREEN'S FARMS AND SAUGATUCK (1648-1933)

Reproduction from the book, Green's Farms, Conn., *by George Penfield Jennings, The Squire of Elmstead, 1933*

Published by The Westport Historical Society 1966

This 1933 map shows the location of the original "long lot" farms given to the Bankside Farmers in 1648. Over the decades, these holdings spread northward toward Weston and west to the Saugatuck River.

This rock in Machamux Park marks the location of one of the native villages of the Paugusset Machamux people, one of the indigenous tribes that lived in the area of Green's Farms for at least 7,500 years prior to colonization by Europeans.

Capt. John Mason's firsthand account of the July 1637 fight between English colonists and Pequots, including Paugusset natives from various local tribes, is pictured here. The Sasco swamp between Green's Farms and modern-day Southport was the site of the final battle of what was known as "the Pequot War" by European colonists. This printed version of Mason's handwritten account was published nearly 100 years later.

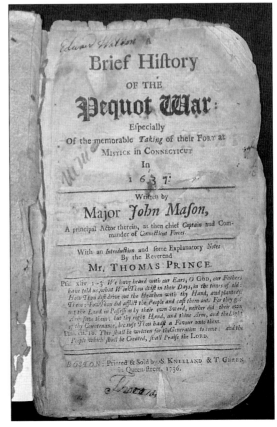

Know all men by these presents, that I Hannah Osborn
of ye Town & County of Fairfield, and Coloney of Connecticut
in New England, for ye Consideration of ye Sum of one
Hundred & five Pounds money of ye province of New york
already recd of Ebenezer Banks of ye Town & County aforesd
Do grant & Convey & Sell into ye sd Ebenezer Banks aforesd
a Certain Negro man named Cesar, about twenty three
years of age, To have and to hold ye above bargained
Premisses, & I ye sd Hannah Osborn do warrent and Defend
ye sd negro man Cesar, against all Claims & molestation
from ~~any~~ all Persons whatsoever, & in Confirmation
whereof I have hereunto Set my hand this 13th Day of
October AD 1761.

In presence of   Hannah osborn

Daniel Osborn
Joseph Osborn

The Osborn family lived on a family compound awarded to ancestor Richard Osborn for serving in the Pequot War. Like other prominent Westport families, they used the labor of enslaved people to manage their large farm. In this deed, Hannah Osborne sold her "negro man" Caesar to fellow Westporter Ebenezer Banks.

Originally located on what is today the Sherwood Island Connector, across the street from the still extant Colonial Cemetery, the Green's Farms Meeting House (later Green's Farms Congregational Church) was burned to the ground by British soldiers in 1779 during the Revolutionary War. (Courtesy Green's Farms Congregational Church.)

Green's Farms Church Lower Cemetery, also called Colonial Cemetery, was founded in 1725 and stood across from the Green's Farms Meeting House of the West Parrish of Fairfield. It is situated close to Long Island Sound between the Post Road and Interstate 95. Abigail Andros's 1730 burial is the oldest interment with a headstone in the graveyard.

The saltbox-style building at the corner of Main Street and Gorham Island Road in this 1930s-era picture was likely built in the late 18th century and was the site of Ebenezer Coley's Saugatuck store and dock. In 1962, it became the Remarkable Book Shop, a beloved town site that closed in 1994.

Two

Westport in the Revolution and Early Republic

In April 1775, George Washington, newly minted commander of the Continental Army, passed through Westport en route to Boston to lead the colonial militia that succeeded in beating back the British at the Battles of Lexington and Concord. He stopped at West Parish Meeting House (Green's Farms Church) to rest and speak with Rev. Hezekiah Ripley about the impending war.

With the Revolution properly begun, Westporters enlisted on both sides. Reverend Ripley would go on to be a chaplain in Washington's army. He ministered to soldiers at Valley Forge. In 1777, British warships moored off Compo beach, landing soldiers en route to Danbury, where patriot munitions and food supplies were stored, ultimately meeting a hostile citizenry and burning the city.

Upon leaving Danbury, the Patriots attacked the British column as it approached Ridgefield, and patriot Brig. Gen. Benedict Arnold temporarily slowed their progress in Ridgefield with a force of 500 men.

The following day, Arnold desperately tried to block the raiders' return to their ships. In a white-knuckle showdown, the British outwitted Arnold by crossing the Saugatuck River at Ford Road and made a mad dash for their ships as Arnold's troops pursued them before being scattered by British bayonet charges on Compo Hill. Included among the 37 patriot soldiers buried at Green's Farm Church is Ebenezer Jesup, a surgeon serving the Continental Army at Valley Forge, as well as Reverend Ripley. In 1779, the British returned and burned the church and parsonage, which stood at what is now the corner of Sherwood Island Connector and Green's Farm Road.

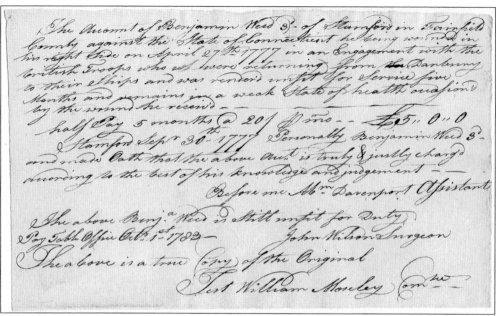

Benjamin Weed of Stamford was injured in a skirmish with British regulars returning to their ships moored at Compo Beach after the raid in Danbury in 1779. This document certified that his injuries prevented him from further service.

The Disbrow Tavern stood on what is now the grounds of Christ & Holy Trinity Church in downtown Westport, its location marked by a plaque. George Washington stopped at the tavern on his way to Lexington and Concord, Massachusetts, in the summer of 1775 to take control of militia forces there.

Cast in bronze by Tiffany & Co., The Minuteman statue near Compo Beach was sculpted by Westport artist H. Daniel Webster, who lived on Sylvan Road. It commemorates the patriot resistance to British forces who landed at Compo on April 25, 1777. This photograph, taken around 1920, shows a sparsely populated neighborhood around the statue, a far cry from how densely developed it is today. The statue was a prominent feature of the final episode of the popular television show *I Love Lucy*.

Green's Farms Congregational Church minister Rev. Hezekiah Ripley met with George Washington in the spring of 1775 when the latter was en route to take command of colonial forces in Massachusetts. Reverend Ripley later served the Continental Army as a chaplain. When the British marched through Westport in 1779 and burned Green's Farms Congregational Church, Ripley and his wife, Abigail, saved this silver communion tankard by placing it in their well. The silver was a gift to the church by Capt. Thomas Hill in 1764. (Courtesy Green's Farms Congregational Church.)

Martha Washington commissioned pitchers to be given to family and friends upon George Washington's death in 1799. These ornate pieces feature the first president with the saying, "Washington in Glory." Production of porcelain in America did not start until the latter half of the 1700s, mostly in Philadelphia. This porcelain pitcher, inscribed with "Rev. H. Ripley," was given to Rev. Hezekiah Ripley, pastor at Green's Farms Church from 1767 to 1821 and Continental Army chaplain. (Courtesy Green's Farms Congregational Church.)

Used as the parsonage of Saugatuck Congregational Church since 1884, Ebenezer Jesup's home was considered the finest mansion in Fairfield County when it was built in 1810. Jesup was a prominent merchant who shipped grain and produce to Boston and owned a store and wharf on the Saugatuck River downtown.

Three

WESTPORT BECOMES AN INDEPENDENT TOWN

For nearly 200 years following the settlement of Green's Farms by the Bankside Farmers in 1648, the area that would eventually become Westport was divided by the Saugatuck River between Fairfield to the east and Norwalk to the west.

With the ending of the war and the creation of the constitution completed in 1818, the state found itself fully immersed in the drive toward an industrial culture, and by 1830, downtown Westport (Saugatuck Village) had become a major shipping center. The residents of this area grew tired of traveling three miles to Green's Farms Congregational Church and decided to build their own church, which was completed in June 1832 as Saugatuck Congregational Church. It was built on the Boston Post Road on land provided by Ebenezer Jesup, a prominent Saugatuck merchant.

After much discussion, the original 36 members of Saugatuck Congregational Church were formally dismissed by letter from the Society of Green's Farms. Saugatuck Congregational Church has thrived since, through the founding of the Town of Westport in 1835, a move of the church across the Post Road in 1950, and a disastrous fire in 2011. Ebenezer Jesup's stately home, built in 1810, was donated to the church for use as the parsonage by his grandson Morris Jesup in 1884; it sits beside the current location of the church.

In 1835, Daniel Nash, a descendant of one of the area's founding families and a prosperous farmer whose land, pond, and grange were on the Norwalk side of the river, got together with others in the town to petition the state legislature to allow an independent town called Westport to be formed. The document stated that most of the petitioners lived beyond the borders of the "town aforesaid" and "a majority of them more than six miles from the place where Town and Electors meetings were always held and the Town Record are always kept and suffer great inconvenience in consequence thereof." The Nash petition went on to say that Norwalk and Fairfield had rival seaports and conflicting interests that made growth and prosperity harder for those who lived between to achieve.

Once accepted by the legislature, Westport was carved out of Weston, Fairfield, and Norwalk and was allowed to levy taxes and be represented by its own board of selectmen. Town meetings were to be held at the "Presbyterian Church," which most likely referred to Saugatuck Congregational Church. The church's charter indicates, "The Society, instituted for the support of the new church, pledged maintenance of public worship, agreeable to the form and all principles of the Presbyterian or Congregational Churches of the United States."

Westport was officially named its own town on May 28, 1835.

This engraving depicts the town of Westport just after its incorporation in 1835. The view is looking west over the wooden drawbridge fording the Saugatuck River downtown. To the right along the riverfront is now Parker Harding plaza. The Christ Church, Episcopal Church is visible on the hill at the intersection of what are today Post and Ludlow Roads, to the left. Consecrated November 2, 1835, it was sold and subsequently torn down after the two Episcopal churches in town combined in 1944 to create the Christ & Holy Trinity Episcopal Church of Westport.

Originally called Green's Farms Academy, the one-room schoolhouse that still stands on Morningside Drive North operated from 1837 to 1867. Two separate entrances and cloakrooms for boys and girls met at a single room for students, warmed by a coal stove. The cupola was removed in the 1960s.

This logbook is written in the hand of Ebenezer Adams, who operated his school, Green's Farms Academy, which became colloquially known as "Adams Academy." The school attracted hundreds of students from near and far, many of whom continued on to Yale. Other students, including E.T. Bedford, went on to attain fame and fortune.

The founder of Green's Farms Academy, Ebenezer Banks Adams hailed from two early Westport families. Educated at Yale University, Adams created a preparatory academy with the express purpose of sending students on to advanced education.

Four

INDUSTRY, INNOVATION, AND INDUSTRIALISTS

In the years immediately after the incorporation of Westport in 1835, progress of various kinds came to the town at a rapid pace. The construction of the New York & New Haven Railroad in 1840 dramatically changed both the landscape and the face of the town. Many of the original railroad construction workers were Irish immigrants who settled in the Saugatuck area. Some 40 years later, Italian immigrants worked on the expansion of the system. From its completion, the railroad rapidly replaced the waterways as the primary method of shipping goods up and down the coast and out to the larger nation. As a result, the vibrant port on the Saugatuck River in what is known today as downtown Westport lost its standing as a commercial hub.

Progress took political and social forms in this era as well, and in 1848, abolition was finalized in Connecticut. In Westport, Lucy and Charles Rowe of Hyde Lane finally achieved their freedom from enslavement. Charles went on to be the sexton at Green's Farms Church, and Lucy is buried in the upper church cemetery. However, while slavery was now illegal in the state, Connecticut firms including clothing and grain mills, ironworks, and other companies continued to do brisk business with the slave-holding south.

When the Civil War began, Westport farmers did their part for the war effort, growing onions as rations for Union soldiers. It was believed that onions, which have mild antimicrobial properties, could prevent infection in open wounds, such as those from gunshots. In fact, Gen. U.S. Grant wrote to the US War Department in Washington, DC, saying that he would not move his troops without a steady supply of onions at his disposal.

After the war's end, Westport also became more appealing to captains of industry and finance. Many wealthy New York families built estates on the shorefront. Among these were the Laurence family, whose lavish home and grounds would one day become Longshore Club Park.

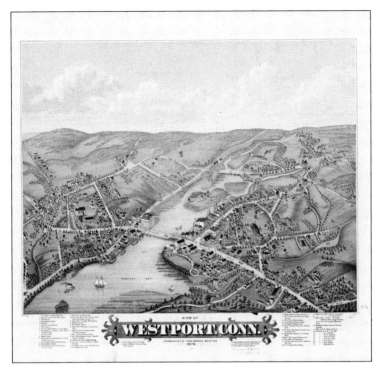

Produced by a sketch artist working from a tethered hot-air balloon at various locations around town, this 1878 view of Westport shows both still extant and long-defunct buildings including various factories, working docks, and Richard H. Winslow's Post Road mansion, Compo House, in what is now Winslow Park.

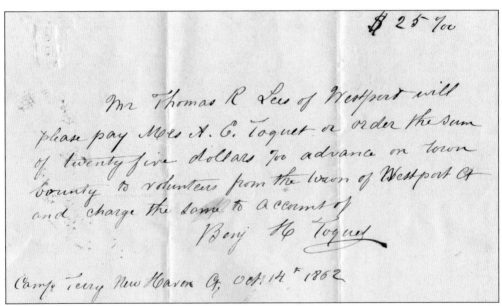

Benjamin H. Toquet was among the Westporters who enlisted in the Union army in return for a $25 bounty raised by the town. This note from Toquet directs Thomas R. Lees to pay his wife, Annie E. Toquet, $25 that was owed him from the town of Westport. Toquet wrote the letter from Camp Terry in New Haven, Connecticut, on Oct. 14, 1862, where he was stationed with Bridgeport Co. I, 23rd Regiment.

The Saugatuck Railroad Bridge provided a thoroughfare for the New York–New Haven line trains to get across the Saugatuck River. The bridge was replaced with newer, modern construction around 1917, and this photograph shows some of the crew. Many of the original railroad construction workers were Irish immigrants who settled around the line's first Westport stop in the Saugatuck area, nicknamed "Little Dublin." Some 40 years later, Italian immigrants worked on the expansion of the system, and Saugatuck quickly became an Italian American enclave called "Little Italy" that thrived for nearly 100 years.

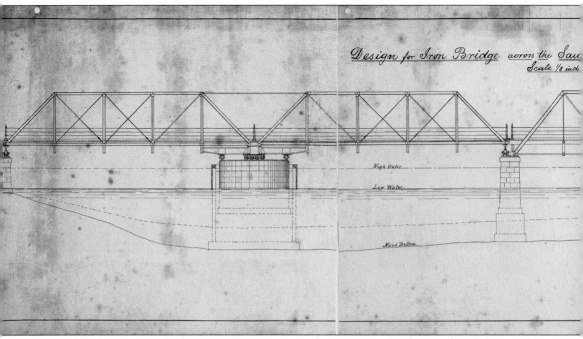

High Water

Low Water

Hard Bottom.

In 1878, the new iron bridge using the most up-to-date swing technology replaced the wooden bridge over the Saugatuck River that had been destroyed by shipworms. The bridge was located just near where the river emptied into Long Island Sound and was, like the railroad, largely built

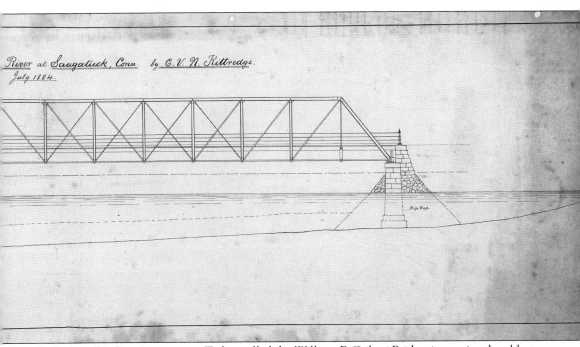

River at Saugatuck, Conn. by E. V. N. Kittredge.
July 1884.

Rip Rap.

by Irish and Italian immigrants. Today, called the William F. Cribari Bridge, it remains the oldest surviving moveable bridge in the state and is listed in the National Register of Historic Places.

The Kemper Tannery stood on the Post Road in a barn originally built by R&H Haight between 1835 and 1837. The company was known as Morocco Manufacturing Co. for a time, with Morocco leather being a firm yet flexible leather that was tanned with sumac or chrome. One of several 19th-century tanneries and leatherworks in the town, the building now houses the Westport Country Playhouse.

In the late 19th and early 20th centuries, factories like the Kemper Tannery employed women, children, and immigrants who did not have the social clout to advocate for fair labor practices—a scenario played out nationwide that eventually led to the rise of labor unions and social reform.

These leatherworkers at the Kemper tannery and men like them worked at one additional tannery in Westport around the turn of the 20th century. Tannery work was messy and odiferous—animal urine was the most common solution used to soften rawhides.

Elonzo S. and Jonathan E. Wheeler's "Button Shop" factory is seen from the Saugatuck River. The buttons were made from "ivory nuts," which were most likely Brazil nut shells. The factory employed children to create the small buttons used on the clothing of the period. Though known as the Button Shop, the official name of the business was the Saugatuck Manufacturing Company. The three houses visible in the background were owned by the Wheelers and stood where Interstate 95 is today.

The Lees Manufacturing Co. in the Richmondville area of town used waterpower to make ribbons, tinsel, twine, cord, and candle wicks and was founded in 1814. The company, shown here in the 1890s, stayed in the Lees family for four generations.

Pine Knoll, Westport, Conn.

This lavish home of the Kemper family stood on the Post Road near their tannery that today houses the Westport Country Playhouse. It later became the Pine Knoll Inn, and following that, a boardinghouse. It was moved to the back of the property to create Playhouse Square until it was torn down to make way for condominiums in the 1980s.

The estate of Standard Oil executive and local philanthropist Edward T. Bedford is seen in Green's Farms. Colloquially called "Nyala Farm," the grounds included a racetrack called Winfromere (or "Win"), where Bedford ran his prized horses. Sherwood Island Connector was built over part of the racetrack.

F.W. Bedford was the brother of Standard Oil executive E.T. Bedford and participated in many of the same businesses. Pictured here is a home on Beachside Avenue fronting Long Island Sound. An avid boater, F.W. Bedford bought an early gas-powered launch from Westport's Toquet Motor Company. (Courtesy Charles Reimer.)

In 1867, Alexander Laurence purchased a 68-acre parcel of land, including what is today the Longshore Club Park, Golf Course, and the Inn at Longshore for $30,000. The Laurences were a wealthy New York City family who owned a home adjacent to Gramercy Park that included stables. Boaters on the sound would have had this view of the house.

The Laurence estate had extensive grounds with ample room for gardens. This photograph shows the statuary in the formal gardens of the estate with Long island Sound in the background.

Maids from Ireland, like Margaret and Ann Gallagher, pictured here with other maids around 1880, as well as African Americans migrating from the American South, worked in the estates around Westport, like the Laurence Estate, which is today Longshore Club Park.

Hockanum was the estate of financier Morris Ketchum on Cross Highway. It was built on property owned by his wife, Caroline Burr. The drives of his 500-acre estate were opened to the public so they might view the work of Ketchum's friend, internationally renowned landscape architect Frederick Law Olmsted, designer of New York's Central Park.

The property at the corner of Post and Compo Roads had been the lavish home of state senator Richard Henry Winslow. The "Winslow Mansion" was extensively renovated in 1853, and the annual firework display on the property brought many visitors to the town. Pres. Millard Fillmore came to Westport in 1859 to discuss Winslow's further political aspirations. In 1891, the property was transferred to the care of Dr. Fredrick D. Ruland for the treatment of the mentally ill at his Westport Sanitarium.

SCHLAET'S PIER, COMPO HILLS, WESTPORT, CONN.

The lavish estate of Arnold Schlaet, co-founder of Texaco, also featured a boathouse on what became known as Schlaet's Point. Known for his extravagant parties during the Jazz Age, Schlaet gave up his 65-foot yacht for use as a submarine chaser during World War I.

Abraham Sherwood's sloop is pictured here in the late 19th century, moored in the Saugatuck River next to the downtown bridge. The building that is now known as National Hall can be seen on the other side of the span. The Sherwoods were farmers who also owned a tide mill at Compo Beach, which milled cracked corn, wheat, and other grains, much of which was sold and transported to the Caribbean to feed planters and their enslaved workers in the 18th century. The Sherwoods remained prominent shipping merchants until the late 19th century.

Captain Frederick Sherwood

Captain Franklin Sherwood

In the mid-19th century, Frederick, Franklin, and Francis Sherwood were triplets who hailed from a 17th-century Westport family. Their father, Daniel, built his home on what is today known as Sherwood Island. When they were not seeking adventures on the high seas in places as far away as Mexico, Africa, Brazil, China, and the Caribbean, the Sherwood triplets, like their ancestors, lived in Westport for the duration of their lives.

Captain Francis Sherwood

Fig. 1.—The Toquet Car.

Westporter Benjamin L. Toquet started out making boats and boat motors; however, in the late 1880s, he became enamored with the automobile. This image appeared in the auto enthusiast magazine *Horseless Age* on August 2, 1905. The Toquet Motor Company produced just a handful of these cars nearly three years before Henry Ford rolled out his Model T. Finding that the market for his car was limited due to high production costs, Toquet turned to specialization and changed the company name to the Toquet Motor and Carburetor Co. The firm began producing carburetors for none other than the Ford Motor Co. as well as smaller models for boat engines.

The unexpected blizzard of 1888 socked in the whole East Coast, with harbors and railways completely grinding to a halt. Snowfall in Connecticut exceeded 50 inches in some places. Here, ice jams water access to the Starch Works on Riverside Avenue.

The *Francis B. Thurber* was a coal barge iced in during a particularly cold snap around 1900. She is pictured here at the Taylor & Richards dock on Riverside Avenue close to downtown. Taylor owned a dry goods store less than a quarter-mile away at the intersection of Riverside Avenue and Post Road.

The weight of snow from the 1888 blizzard collapsed the wooden bridge that carried the Post Road (State Street) over the Saugatuck River. The bridge was replaced by a concrete structure soon thereafter. National Hall is clearly visible on the opposite side.

In this unusual view of Main Street looking south toward the Post Road (State Street), snowfall from the Blizzard of 1888 has made the road impassable. The blizzard caused so much widespread damage that it is still considered one of the greatest storms to ever hit New England.

Five

AROUND THE TOWN

Following the Civil War, towns like Westport, ideally situated on the coast and serviced by new railway systems, found themselves in the midst of growing prosperity. In Westport, men like Horace Staples, who was destined to become the wealthiest man in town, used their means for public as well as private improvement projects, such as the building of the first public high school in town, which carries his name to this day.

Westport's landscape rapidly changed as modern factories cropped up from Saugatuck to what is now the Richmondville area of the town. These included two tanneries and multiple cotton mills. A new iron bridge using the most up-to-date swing technology replaced the wooden drawbridge over the Saugatuck River, just near where it empties into Long Island Sound. Today called the William F. Cribari Bridge, it remains the oldest surviving moveable bridge in the state. By 1878, the town was densely populated, with the downtown area closely resembling what it is today, although the nature of commerce has shifted to retail.

The second half of the 19th century was also a dizzying era of invention, technology, and wealth. Westport's robber baron industrialists made fortunes on new technologies and even bigger manufacturing concerns. For the first time, women could work out of the home without social reprobation, usually in factory settings and often alongside children. In Westport, the manufactories that dotted the Saugatuck River expanded, including the Embalmer's Supply Company and Baynham Coffin Tack factory—capitalizing on new advancements that even affected the way people presented and mourned the dead.

In addition to social activism, a renewed interest in the arts and history grew during this era, and literary and art salons, as well as common interest societies, flourished. In 1886, the Westport Reading Room & Lending Library was formed to bring the gift of literature to all Westporters, and in 1889, the Westport Historical Society (later renamed the Saugatuck Historical Society, and then changed back again) was formed by members of the town's founding families. Today, the organization is known as the Westport Museum for History & Culture.

This 1896 view of the Post Road looking east features the electric trolley that replaced the horse-drawn omnibus that provided public transportation through the town. The building to the right still stands today. The Sherwood house is visible behind the trolley at the corner of Post Road and Church Lane. It was moved farther down Church Lane and is now a restaurant.

Tall trees no longer line the sidewalks of Main Street looking north, but the road still remains a retail thoroughfare. A beer garden and saloon stand in the right-hand corner of this photograph. It was later torn down to make room for the Bedford YMCA.

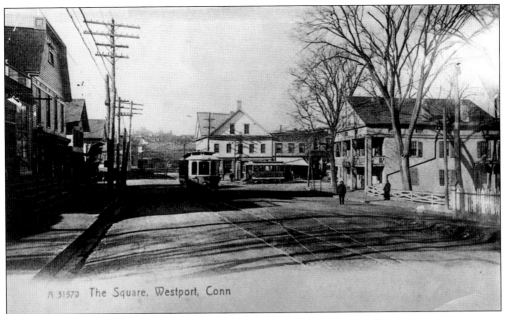

Clear-cut farmland can be seen over the bridge at the far end of this view of Hotel Square. The Toquet Opera House, with its reverse trapezoid-shaped roof, faces the Westport Hotel, later replaced by the YMCA built by industrialist E.T. Bedford.

The Westport Hotel, a popular spot, particularly for beachgoers visiting Westport, is seen in this c. 1910 view. This early motorcar might have belonged to a prominent guest.

From the mid-19th century through the turn of the 20th century, the express horse-drawn trolley escorted travelers from the Westport Hotel, downtown on the Post Road, directly to the Saugatuck Train Station.

At the beginning of the 20th century, an electric trolley replaced the horse-drawn omnibus that traveled throughout points town-wide, including the Westport and Green's Farm train stations.

The electric trolley that provided public transportation throughout Westport was stored in a shed next to the old Westport Hotel. It was torn down, along with the hotel, to build the Bedford YMCA, which was completed in 1923.

Westport Library. *Dear Julia I received your postal and thank you for the same.* Helen Walter

In 1906, the 10-year-old Westport Reading Room and Lending Library was improved by Morris K. Jesup, who funded a new building in the heart of downtown next to the Saugatuck River. Jesup's library was an impressive brick and granite building that employed elements of classical Greek and Roman architecture. Today, the space has been home to various retail stores.

Interior Westport Library

The Jesup library featured electric lighting and an impressive marble fireplace for members' maximum reading comfort when it opened its doors in 1908. The library operated at this site, which featured a carved lintel that read, "Open To All," until 1986, when the new building overlooking Jesup Green was constructed.

Shercrowe School operated for nearly 100 years from the early 1800s to the beginning of the 20th century in the section of town that was once part of Norwalk. Originally called the West Saugatuck District School, the one- (and later two-) room schoolhouse provided students basic education. Shercrowe School was at one time the only school in Westport and operated until 1905. Today, the building is a private home. The lone African American student in the photograph is Anna Sims.

This c. 1890s photograph, taken from a Main Street window, shows the Bradley Wheeler Dry Goods & Hardware store on the south side of the Post Road standing beside the trapezoidal roofed Toquet Opera House, which was built in 1892. The opera house was on the second floor while the first floor housed town records until the town hall was built in 1908. The electric trolley and the horse-watering basin at the intersection of Main Street are visible as well.

R. Ferrara's Block, Westport, Conn.

Proprietor Rosano Ferrara was a member of the growing Italian immigrant community in Westport. His grocery store sold fresh produce, dairy, and treats like Coca-Cola. The top of the Jesup Library is just visible at upper left.

The Masiello family owned a 5¢, 10¢, and 25¢ store on Main Street as well as a farm at their Cross Highway home, which later featured a country store opened by Christine Masiello in the 1920s. This early 1900 photograph shows Masiello family members in front of the store.

Strawberry pickers are pictured at Masiello's farm on Cross Highway in 1920. Immigrants from Europe and African Americans migrating from the South often found work as farmhands. The Masiellos were one of the town's many Italian families.

William E. Nash operated the drugstore he owned, Nash's Apothecary and Patent Medicine, out of No. 4 Hurlbutt Building from the late 19th to the early 20th century. Nash sold common drugs and everyday items of convenience, such as brooms, soap, and penny candies from his candy counter, which attracted kids from all over town. He also capitalized on the location of the post office just next door and began selling postcards depicting scenes of the town starting in the early 1900s.

First home of the First National Bank, Westport, Conn.

Industry boomed in Westport in the 19th century thanks to the arrival of the railroad. Factories popped up on the shores of the Saugatuck River, and banks offered their services to businesses in need. The Saugatuck Bank stood where National Hall is today.

STERN, BROOKLYN, N. Y.   HULBERT'S BLOCK, WESTPORT, CONN.

a postal from Johnie to Frank.

The Hurlbutt Building was a two-story brick structure that stood approximately at the site of today's two-story brick Gault Building between Jesup Road and Taylor Place on State Street (the Post Road). Built in the early 1860s, the building housed a variety of businesses and public institutions over the years, including the Westport Post Office and William E. Sturges and Sons' shoe sales and repair shop.

In 1934, a blizzard blocked access to the storefronts on Main Street, including Westport Hardware, which was located next to Greenberg's department store on the west side of the street. (Courtesy Charles Reimer.)

The Westport Sanitarium, under the supervision of Dr. Frederick D. Ruland, first opened in 1891 at the corner of Post Road East and Compo Road North. Prior to being a sanitarium, the property had been the lavish home of state senator Richard Henry Winslow.

Leo Ruland, Dr. Frederick Ruland's wife, was an avid amateur photographer who extensively cataloged life at Westport Sanitarium, which her husband founded, and in the town at large. She took many photographs, like this one, of staff and sanitarium grounds workers. (Courtesy Charles Reimer.)

Dr. McFarland opened McFarland's Sanitarium and operated as head physician in 1898. McFarland's Sanitarium was later renamed Hall-Brooke Sanitarium in the 1960s and later Hall-Brooke Foundation. This building was torn down in 2003, and the grounds are now the site of a Level IV trauma center of St. Vincent's Hospital.

Mary Frances Pearson Porter was about two years old when this photograph was taken in 1919. The Bradley-Wheeler House, headquarters of the Westport Museum, can be seen behind her. Her father, Robert L. Pearson, was a diver who worked for the New Haven Railroad.

This is a view of Church Lane in the late 19th century taken from the corner of Elm Street looking east toward Myrtle Avenue. Very little has changed from this photograph except for the addition of some more buildings and paving on the roads.

The Guyer & Sons building on the south side of the Post Road at the corner of Taylor Place sold dry goods, including ammunition, which exploded during a fire that destroyed the store around 1920 when it was owned by the Gault Company. The new store was built across Taylor Place and today houses Tiffany & Co.

The Gault Company, located on Riverside Avenue in Saugatuck, sold coal and building supplies, including lumber, and had a hauling business. This 1910 photograph shows the building, various employees, and wagons.

Built in the Classical Revival style, Westport's original town hall building is unique in its use of cobblestones as a building material. Listed in the National Register of Historic Places, it was built in 1908 and was the town's first official town hall and first all-purpose municipal building. In 1979, Westport Town Hall was relocated to the old Bedford Elementary School opposite Veterans Green on Myrtle Avenue. Today, Old Town Hall houses offices, restaurants, and retail establishments.

The Italianate Bradley Wheeler House was built in 1865 by Morris Bradley. It replaced a five-bay second period Colonial house, which stood on the site when it was owned by Ebenezer Coley of Coleytown. At various times in its history, the lower floors housed medical offices and other businesses. It is today the headquarters of the Westport Museum.

Standing on the property of the Westport Museum, this seven-sided cobblestone milking barn was built in 1846. At one time, stables stood alongside the structure. Underneath the barn is an icehouse accessible by subterranean steps as well as a trap door inside the structure. Listed in the National Register of Historic Places, the barn is unique in Connecticut and one of the few in New England.

The Bradley Wheeler Hardware and Sporting Goods Store, on the south side of Post Road, is decked out in patriotic bunting in 1905. Frederick Bradley was the proprietor and also advertised general electrical repair services.

In the late 19th and early 20th centuries, the Lehn family operated a bakery on the west side of Main Street close to Post Road, which had coal-fed ovens at the back of the building. The bakery sold bread as well as cake, donuts, cream puffs, and other treats.

In 1919, the concrete bridge spanning the Saugatuck River at the Post Road featured a small building where the mechanism to lift the drawbridge was housed. The marshy area in the foreground is now a public parking lot. National Hall is in the distance. (Courtesy Charles Reimer.)

Horace Staples opened the Saugatuck Bank in the Saugatuck section of town in 1852 but moved it "uptown" to the new building that stood on the northwest side of the Post Road bridge. He renamed it the First National Bank & Trust, which later became Westport Bank & Trust in 1913. The building housed Westport Furniture in the mid-20th century, and later a boutique hotel called National Hall.

Taken around 1906, this view of the Post Road looking east was likely from the higher elevations of Wright Street. The then-new public library building is visible across the river, dominating the skyline of downtown.

The King's Highway was one of the original colonial roads in the town and remains a busy residential thoroughfare today. When this postcard was made in the early 1900s, it was still a dirt road. The house on the left is Sunbright, belonging to one of Westport's oldest families, the Nashes. (Courtesy Charles Reimer.)

VIEW ON KING ST., WESTPORT, CONN.

Prior to 1884, Westport students had to travel out of town to pursue a high school education. Horace Staples, a descendant of one of the town's prominent founding families, had a lifelong dream of building a high school in Westport. While he himself had only a few years of formal education, he had worked briefly as a teacher, ultimately becoming a successful local businessman. In 1884, he provided the land and funding to build Staples High School in its original location on Riverside Avenue, not far from his own home. The site today is Saugatuck Elementary School.

From 1900 to 1912, student enrollment in Westport's public schools rose by 30 percent, prompting the construction of new school buildings, including Bedford Elementary School in 1917, which was funded by a major contribution by industrialist E.T. Bedford. The school operated until the late 1970s, when it was renovated for use as Westport Town Hall.

The Rippe Orchards stretched from Turkey Hill Road north to Long Lots Road and featured a farm stand on the corner of Post and Turkey Hill Roads, which also had a cider press. The stand was torn down to make way for Harvest Commons Condominiums in the 1980s.

Originally a bamboo hut built for the Philippine exhibit at the St. Louis Fair in 1904, this building was dismantled and reconstructed by Herman Bumpus soon thereafter at Compo Mill Cove, where it still stands today in much-renovated form.

This 1920s photograph of young Harold McGill roasting peanuts at about 12 years old was taken in front of Wagner's Saloon at the corner of Wilton Road and Post Road. At left is Tony Chichisola's fruit store and soda fountain.

The Vigilant Engine Company 3 on Wilton Road, just north of the Post Road intersection, was formed in 1864. The building remains as a restaurant site. Here, firefighters and their canine mascot display full regalia at a town parade in the 1910s.

At the turn of the 20th century, the firefighters from Engine Company 4 in Saugatuck pulled their wagon-mounted hoses by hand. The company was first formed in 1832.

The Pioneer Ladder Company in downtown Westport, also known as Compo Engine Company, founded in 1859, is seen above in 1935 and below in 1955. It was located next to the Bedford YMCA and is today part of a retail complex. The firehouse relocated to Post Road slightly outside of central downtown.

Dr. Sherwood served as a general practitioner in the town and health officer until 1909. Here, he is making house calls by sleigh in the aftermath of the Blizzard of 1888.

The Great New England Hurricane of 1938 wrought catastrophic damage up and down the East Coast. Flooding carried away cars and inundated homes as the waters of Long Island Sound rose at Saugatuck Shores, as pictured here.

Frank Esposito's service station was in Saugatuck on Charles Street. He supplied commuters with taxis as well as a place for others to park their cars.

First National Supermarkets owned three stores in Westport at one time. This one, seen in the 1940s, is the current location of Trader Joe's in the Compo Shopping Center along Post Road East.

Hubbell & Bradley was located in Saugatuck, with its coal yard on Riverside Avenue. Their office and storehouse, seen here, was on Railroad Avenue. The company advertised a fireproof storage warehouse and sold coal, feed, and mason's building supplies and provided motor and horse trucking services.

At the turn of the 20th century, horses and wagons shared downtown roads with electric and gasoline-powered automobiles as well as new electric trolleys. Farming families were often seen driving their horse-drawn wagons down the roadways well into the 20th century.

Up until 1950, the Saugatuck River flowed right up to the back of the Main Street stores, just as it did when 18th- and 19th-century merchants had loading docks for sloops carrying goods to Long Island Sound. The area was filled in to create the Parker Harding public parking lot.

A snowstorm snarls traffic going east from Norwalk across the Wilton Road in 1934. The building to the left still stands today. (Courtesy Charles Reimer.)

Even the dawn of a powerfully mechanized age could not stop Mother Nature, and in 1888, a historic blizzard hit the East Coast and Connecticut particularly hard, wreaking havoc throughout the state and derailing railway cars. The New Haven line train was halted in Green's Farms, where snow piles blocked the tracks. It took eight days to dig out the rails by hand.

This image shows a member of the Seaver family on a country lane in Westport in the late 19th century.

This 1860 Italianate-style house was moved from Main Street during a period of commercial redistricting in the early 1960s to this site on Gorham Island. It was torn down in the 1970s.

Saugatuck Congregational Church, built in 1832, was moved across the street from its original location on the Post Road in 1950. The undertaking was so delicate that the event made the cover of *Life* magazine.

**Methodist Episcopal Church
Westport, Conn.**

PUBLISHED BY W. E. NASH, WESTPORT, CONN

Appearing on the 1878 map of Westport, the Methodist Episcopal Church faced Main Street from the corner of Myrtle Avenue. It was sold in 1945 and torn down at some point thereafter. Wheeler House, headquarters of the Westport Museum, is just visible in the right background.

The doughboy memorial statue commemorating Westporters' service in World War I by local illustrator and sculptor J. Clinton Shepherd was erected on Post Road on November 11, 1930. The statue was later moved and now stands in Veteran's Green across from town hall and next door to the Westport Museum.

At 1:25 a.m. on Friday, September 27, 1935, the unthinkable happened when freight trains crashed on the railroad bridge over the Saugatuck River. The crash between the two high-speed trains was so loud that it was heard throughout the town, and it took firefighters from Westport, Norwalk, and Fairfield hours to get the resulting fire under control.

Six

RECREATION

Compo Beach and Long Island Sound have always been integral parts of life in Westport. During the area's earliest native settlements, the shores of Compo, which meant "the bear's fishing ground," provided clams, oysters, and other fishing opportunities, which European colonizers later took advantage of. During colonial times and well into the early 20th century, the waters of the sound functioned as a bustling and protected thoroughfare for shipping traffic from New York City past the Connecticut/Rhode Island border and all the way to Canada.

As shipping waned in the late 19th century, oystering remained a prominent and healthy business in the waters of Long Island Sound, including in Westport, where family oyster businesses still work the waters today. Recreational oystering and clamming were popular pastimes then as now.

At the same time, pleasure-bathing joined picnicking as a leisure activity for Westporters and out-of-town visitors. The large and commodious pavilion at Compo Beach provided shade and refreshment to beachgoers, who were protected in their swims by the professional lifeguard corps that worked there.

Those staying longer than a day's outing could stay at one of the many inns that popped up around the town and at the shore from the mid-19th century throughout the 21st, although the golden age of hospitality in Westport largely occurred from the early 1900s to about 1970.

Boating and sailing also continue to be popular off the shores at Compo Beach, as the two town marinas attest.

In a scene still played out today, Florence Newman (right) and her fellow picnickers enjoy Westport's Compo Beach around the turn of the 20th century.

Summertime at Westport's Compo Beach has changed little over the centuries, with crowds of bathers filling the sandy shore, taking respite between swims in Long Island Sound.

Wheeled changing rooms, like this one at Compo Beach, were popular in the late 19th and early 20th century as a way to allow people to modestly change into bathing costumes and then wade out into the water.

While today the lifeguard corps at Compo Beach is mostly teenagers, in the early 1900s, the corps was made up of adult men. Their large number attests to the constant influx of bathers visiting Compo Beach even 100 years ago.

Located on Beachside Avenue, the Beachside Inn started out as a private home. Its ample verandas with views of Long Island Sound made it a popular spot for vacationers.

CLUB HOUSE DINING TERRACE

Before the town of Westport bought the former Laurence estate and turned it into Longshore Club Park in 1960, there was Longshore Beach & Country Club, a private club where elite members could enjoy dining, dancing, and swimming.

For much of the town's settlement, the Saugatuck River was an industrial waterway servicing merchants and factories along its shores. By the 1950s, most heavy industry had departed, and the river became a popular spot for pleasure boaters.

This concept drawing of what is today Bedford Square depicts the original site of the Westport YMCA, which was funded by Westporter and steel magnate Edward Thomas Bedford. Almost completely faithful to the final build, the site is easily recognizable today at the corner of Main Street and the Post Road. The Westport Hotel, a popular way station for travelers and beachgoers, was torn down to make way for the YMCA, which remained in these quarters from 1923 until 2015.

SHERWOOD ISLAND STATE PARK
Westport, Connecticut

In the early years of the 20th century, state parks were opening all over America and provided free or low-cost places for people to gather and enjoy nature. In Westport, Sherwood Island State Park opened in 1932, and bathers from Westport and beyond could spend a day in the sun to escape the gloomy outlook of the Depression years.

In operation from 1950 to 1981, the Clam Box Restaurant was part of a small chain and a Westport staple. They served traditional New England–style baked, boiled, and fried seafood and chowders.

Robert Frawley owned the liquor store on Main Street, and his partner John Sullivan operated a café in the small adjoining space. This building still stands today, though it no longer sells liquor.

On the Weston-Westport border, the Cobbs Mill Inn, which opened in 1936, was beloved by members of both communities. It was a favorite spot for watching ducks, and the waterfall flow was beautiful when the stream level was high enough for the full cascade effect. Countless weddings, parties, and events were held there over the years until its closure in 2016.

Hawthorne Inn,
Westport, Conn.

The Hawthorne Inn occupied the southeast corner of the Post Road at Compo Road. It was demolished to make way for the Compo Acres shopping center.

First known as the Open Door Hotel, the General Putnam Inn was a downtown hotel that offered rooms for African American servants traveling with their employers. Demolished to make way for municipal buildings in the latter half of the 20th century, the General Putnam Inn was located on Jesup Green. It was one of the in-town hotels and inns that served the many business and recreational visitors to the town.

Now known as the Westport Inn, the New Englander Motor Hotel advertised 76 rooms and suites, air conditioning, TVs, radios, a restaurant, and cocktail lounge as well as party rooms, a cabana club, swimming pool, and putting greens. Many of these amenities are still available today.

Allen's Clam House was located at the Compo Mill Pond (also known as Sherwood Mill Pond and Old Mill Pond) and was an icon among Westport eateries. Proprietor Capt. Walter Allen was one of a long line of Westport sailors. Ernest LaFrance, pictured here, was a regular customer.

A multi-generational Westporter, Capt. Walter Allen was a recognizable and beloved figure in town. Here, he is shucking oysters for his restaurant, Allen's Clam House, which stood at the site of the current public park at the Compo Mill Cove.

Allen's Clam House was noted for its views of the Compo Mill Pond and Long Island Sound as much as for its chowder, which one *New York Times* reviewer called "extremely satisfying." Food was served in a "long dining room . . . designed to give as much picture-window space to the star of the show—the water—as possible."

Once known as the Club Grill, Muriel's Trolley Car Diner sold traditional diner fare. Westporters would go to the Trolley Car Diner for their favorite meals, and kids could play the much-loved pinball machine at the back. The restaurant burned in 1974, along with the building next to it.

Located on the Post Road near the Fairfield border, the Greyhound Post House was a 1925 building that was also a Greyhound bus station. It later became the Pepper Mill Steak and Fish House. It was torn down in 2007. Goodwill Industries now occupies the site.

The crowds at Compo Beach have always been an issue, but excellent trolley service was once used to transport people from the beach back to downtown Westport and even to the railroad station.

Bathing House, Compo Beach, Westport, Conn.

Built in the late 19th century, the Compo Pavilion had showers, changing rooms, and public areas for day visitors to Compo Beach.

Westport Sanitarium founder Dr. Frederick Ruland had a home on the site of his hospital grounds and a beach house at Compo Mill Cove, along with a seaplane, shown here in 1935. (Courtesy Charles Reimer.)

Memorial Cannons, Campo Beach, Westport, Conn.

Installed July 1, 1901, to commemorate the British landing at Compo Beach in April 1777 at the onset of the Revolutionary War, the Compo Beach cannons immediately became and remained a popular tourist spot, meeting destination, and play area for children.

The lure of the calm, cool waters at Compo Beach has long attracted visitors to get their ankles wet. These beachgoers were members or guests of the Laurence family, who owned a large estate on the water that later became the town of Westport's Longshore Club Park.

YACHT CLUB BASIN, WESTPORT, CONN.

The yacht basin near Compo Beach was one of two marinas owned by the town. Pleasure boaters could rent slips for the season or for single-day docking.

These late-19th-century photographs identify Mr. and Mrs. Fisher (left) and the dapper Edgar Van Horn (below) pursuing recreational clamming on Westport shores.

One of the few restaurants fronting the Saugatuck riverfront in the downtown area during the 20th century, the Mooring Restaurant building was constructed in 1900. The current occupant is Rive Bistro.

THE MOORING RESTAURANT

Labor Day in Westport has always been synonymous with Compo Beach, and 100 years ago, the lifeguards held water sports competitions and other amusements. The *Westporter-Herald* advertised a much-anticipated greased watermelon race as well as swimming races. Swimmers from Stamford to Bridgeport were expected to arrive and challenge the Compo lifeguards. The American Band of Norwalk was hired to play a concert, and even a hydroplane was on hand to take revelers to the skies.

In the late 19th and early 20th century, clubs like the largely Italian St. Anthony's Society of Saugatuck held an annual festival honoring its patron saint. The event waned as second-generation Italian Westporters had become fully "Americanized," but in 1980, it was revived as the Festival Italiano and continued for nearly another 30 years.

Originally known as the Old Mill Grocery & Deli, this small grocer provided staples to beach residents who did not want to take the longer trek into town. Later known as Elvira's, it functioned for many decades as a small deli until it closed in 2018 and reopened in 2019 as Elvira Mae's.

Seven

WESTPORT IN THE ARTS

Westport's bucolic beauty has long attracted creatives of all kinds, including visual artists and writers. F. Scott Fitzgerald penned his masterpiece *The Great Gatsby* while summering in Westport in 1920. Noted horror and mystery short story writer Shirley Jackson lived in the town briefly during the 1940s, as did children's author and illustrator Robert Lawson, whose work *The Story of Ferdinand*, published in 1936, later became the Disney favorite *Ferdinand the Bull*.

Artists including George Hand Wright, who moved here at the turn of the 20th century, illustrator and WPA artist Robert Lambdin, sculptor J. Clinton Shepherd, magazine illustrator Stevan Dohanos, and artist and civil rights activist Tracy Sugarman, among others, lived and worked in Westport. They were part of a vibrant art community that spanned nearly 100 years as evidenced by the many *New Yorker* magazine covers painted by Westport artists or depicting the town.

The Famous Artists School, a correspondence-based arts and writing program, headquartered in Westport from 1948 to 1972, included Norman Rockwell among its founding faculty along with Harold Von Schmidt and others. Through its various programs, average Americans could try their hand at becoming artists.

From music to film to stage, Westport has long attracted performers and supported the performing arts. In 1892, Benjamin Toquet founded the Toquet Opera House on land inherited by his wife. Musical conductor Leonard Bernstein lived just over the Westport line in Fairfield, and during the 1960s, gave charity concerts for civil rights activities at Staples High School. The high school also hosted numerous rock bands in the 1960s, including the Doors. Since 1973, the Levitt Pavilion in downtown Westport has provided free summer-long concerts by notable musicians and paid benefit concerts by music industry megastars.

Early silent-film star W.S. Hart called the town home, as did golden age of cinema greats, including Paul Newman and Joanne Woodward, Bette Davis, Eartha Kitt, and many more. The final season of TV's beloved series *I Love Lucy* was set in Westport as well.

In 1931, Lawrence Langner, a New York theater producer, opened the Westport Country Playhouse in C.H. Kemper's old tannery as a summer stock theater where stars of Broadway and film could hone their skills with workshop productions. Notable actors including Paul Robeson, Helen Hayes, and Ethel Barrymore have graced the Playhouse stage over its nine decades.

Kewpie doll creator Rose O'Neill lived in Westport and is seen here in the 1920s, posing with her creations. O'Neill was considered quite bohemian, and an ardent supporter of women's suffrage.

This group photograph of Famous Artists School instructors includes Norman Rockwell (left of center, with bow tie and pipe), among its founding faculty, along with Harold Von Schmidt (seated in left background, wearing a fedora) and others.

In 1907, George Hand Wright, a prominent engraver, illustrator, and painter, purchased the house at 93 Cross Highway for himself and his wife, Anne Boylan. In fact, Wright often joked that the bulk of the renovations he did at his home, which was built in 1764, were done specifically to accommodate the many guests who had come to visit them in the country.

Opened in 1931, the Westport Country Playhouse, the summer stock home of the New York Repertory Company, provided a distraction for Westporters struggling during the Great Depression. Notable and up-and-coming actors tested out Broadway-bound shows and other performances on audiences eager for diversion—all for a fraction of a New York City show's ticket price.

Benjamin Louis Toquet's father, Benjamin H., immigrated to Westport from France in 1845, and in 1892, Benjamin Louis opened the Westport Opera House, now known as Toquet Hall; recognizable by its trapezoidal roof, it remains a venue for teens to practice performing arts.

In the summer of 1920, the celebrated young writer F. Scott Fitzgerald, a key figure of the Jazz Age, and his glamorous young wife, Zelda, sought respite from their whirlwind lives and rented an 18th-century farmhouse on Long Island Sound near the estate of multi-millionaire Frederick Lewis, which is today Longshore Club Park. In this idyllic Westport location, Scott took advantage of the bucolic quiet to work on what he hoped would be his next great novel—*The Great Gatsby*. (Courtesy Princeton University Library.)

<table>
<tr><td>

Sec'y. Treas. &
Official Shock Absorber
KAY PAINTON

</td><td>

Office Help &
Hindrances
BUDDY & CINDERS

</td></tr>
</table>

FREDERICK C. PAINTON, INC.
Official Receiver
FOR FLOPS AND DEPRESSION OF 1932
Receiving Barns located at Rayfield Place, Westport, Conn.

RECEIVED FROM ....
All 1932 flops, flat tires, headaches and busted aspira-
tions for which we herewith send you

    One Set .... **Brand new hopes**

    One Ton .... **Renewed faith**

    (Above items for use in New Year of 1933)
This corporation also extends its fervent Christmas
wishes and good will.

....
             President

This holiday card from Westport-based cartoonist Frederick C. Painton wryly offers to accept recipients' troubles in return for a measure of hope. Light-hearted—if sarcastic—holiday greetings were one of the many ways those suffering through the Great Depression tried to put a good face on a bad situation.

The Fine Arts Theater on Main Street opened in 1920 and was separated from the original town hall by a walkway. It seated over 700 people. Today, the building is the site of Restoration Hardware.

Westporter Paul Newman often participated in fundraisers at Westport Museum when it was the Westport Historical Society. Locals delighted in seeing the international film star serving drinks or flipping burgers on the lawn of the organization's headquarters, the Bradley-Wheeler House.

DISCOVER THOUSANDS OF LOCAL HISTORY BOOKS FEATURING MILLIONS OF VINTAGE IMAGES

Arcadia Publishing, the leading local history publisher in the United States, is committed to making history accessible and meaningful through publishing books that celebrate and preserve the heritage of America's people and places.

Find more books like this at
www.arcadiapublishing.com

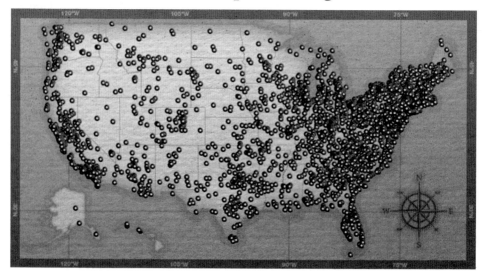

Search for your hometown history, your old stomping grounds, and even your favorite sports team.